D0467907

Southern Living

SECRETS OF

Style

Southern Living®
SECRETS OF
Style

Oxmoor
House®

Oxmoor House, Inc.
Editor in Chief: Nancy Fitzpatrick Wyatt
Executive Editor: Susan Carlisle Payne
Art Director: Cynthia Rose Cooper
Copy Chief: Allison Long Lowery

Southern Living At HOME
Senior Vice President and Executive Director: Dianne Mooney
Director of Design: Melanie Grant

Southern Living® Secrets of Style
Editor: Rebecca Brennan
Contributing Editor: Susan Ray
Copy Editor: Jacqueline Giovanelli
Contributing Copy Editor: L. Amanda Owens
Editorial Assistant: Terri Laschober
Director of Production: Phillip Lee
Associate Production Manager: Leslie Wells Johnson
Production Assistant: Faye Porter Bonner

Contributors
Designer: Rita Yerby
Intern: Amber Ballew

Oxmoor House®

For more books to enrich your life, visit
oxmoorhouse.com

contents

Foreword

*H*ome . . . what a wonderful word! It's a refuge and a sanctuary that embraces you each time you enter. It's a place where wonderful memories are made to enjoy now and to pass along to future generations. Home *is* where the heart is. And with this beautiful volume from the homes editors and photo stylists at *Southern Living* magazine, we hope you'll find imaginative ideas to help you create style, comfort, ease, and a feeling of welcome that makes your home a haven for all to enjoy.

Dianne

Dianne Mooney

Founder, *Southern Living At HOME*

Introduction

Would you jump at the chance to spend an afternoon with one of the talented stylists at *Southern Living* magazine? Just think of all the decorating

questions you could ask! And all the quick and easy decorating secrets you'd learn! Many of our readers have wished that they could invite our design experts into their homes . . . and now you can have the next best thing. In this beautiful book, we've brought together the best ideas, techniques, and tricks of the trade *Southern Living* has to offer.

Take a walk with us through the color-filled pages and lose yourself in the possibilities. . . . Whether you want to transform your home, top to bottom, or make a room your own with a few special touches, our *Southern Living* decorators are here to help you with a wealth of creative ideas, inspiration, and advice. Learn how to mix fabric and textures for maximum impact, arrange treasures on your wall, and group your collections in eye-catching ways. No matter what you dream of doing, this book will give you the know-how to meet your design challenges with confidence.

Melanie

Melanie Grant

Director of Design, *Southern Living At HOME*

gathering rooms

For more on this living room, see page 19.

welcoming
entryways

The entryway or foyer sets the tone for the rest of your home. It's the first room your friends and family will see, so make a great first impression. This space can be purely decorative. A group of prints hung together makes a big impact on bare walls, as well as provides a focal point. If space is limited, use furniture that provides storage. A small chest is ideal for keeping keys, hats, and gloves organized. Here are some other secrets for helping this area achieve its full potential.

• Define an open entryway with a rug.

• Accessorize with an attractive basket to collect mail or papers.

• A console table is a good furnishing solution for a small entry. The narrow dimensions create a more spacious look.

• Flank a table or chest with a pair of side chairs. The chairs can be used in other areas of your home when additional seating is needed.

• Mix traditional furnishings with more contemporary accessories or artwork.

Julie Feagin Sandner
Assistant Homes Editor, *Southern Living*

Make a strong impact in the foyer by prominently displaying pieces of art and furniture that share a mood. **Go with the Flow:** Utilize color, fabrics, and art to create a cohesive look from room to room. Here, the wall color, warm-hued rugs, and the golden tones of wood and wicker connect the entryway and dining area. **Feast for Your Eyes:** Artwork brings this room's design together. The prints in the foyer direct attention to the dining room wall where similarly framed art hangs. **Pure and Simple:** (inset) The use of artwork as a unifying decoration is seen again with prints hung above an iron table. Keep accents to a minimum in the entry; additional accessorizing detracts from the art.

"Unexpected combinations create a welcoming environment. Here, exterior lanterns highlight the hand-painted bench below." **Julie Feagin Sandner**

Given the entryway's prominence, wall color, furniture, and accessories have the opportunity to make big first impressions. **The Right Stuff:** Use a variety of pieces to form a design theme in the foyer. The painted bench, outdoor lanterns, and mirror create a cozy French provincial feel. The herringbone-patterned brick flooring and V-groove paneling distinguish the entry from the rest of the house. **Small Comfort:** A luxuriously detailed pillow resting in the corner of the bench introduces pattern and texture and adds an inviting touch.

Think of the wall space in the foyer as an opportunity to add an individual touch, such as an interesting collection. **Opening Statement:** The narrow focus of an entry hall provides a perfect venue for a wall display. In this space, assorted botanical prints in a variety of gold frames command center stage. A neutral wall color allows the art to really pop, while the common theme of the prints and the similar framing makes the arrangement work as an impressive unit. **Base Note:** An antique marble-and-iron console is an elegant foundation for the wall grouping. Small lamps—something to consider in an entryway without much natural light—offer a bright note.

In a foyer, relate the color palette to the adjoining rooms. **Pleasing Accents:** For this open floor plan, the neutral wall color works well to connect the foyer with the rest of the house. Pillows and upholstery fabrics in bright colors spark interest. A well-chosen rug can introduce the home's color scheme, setting the stage for what's to come. **Sitting Pretty:** An arched window seat just inside the entrance offers an intriguing hideaway. The mix of sconces and recessed lights makes the area appear bright and warm.

A small foyer is large on personality with a few well-chosen accents. **Mirror, Mirror:** A large mirror resting on the floor reflects the front door and visually doubles the space. **Point of Interest:** A stack of pillows gives a low ottoman additional height and contributes interesting color and texture underneath the table. **Bright Idea:** Unusual accessories, such as these lamps, add personality and pizzazz to the area.

tasteful & stylish
living rooms

To distinguish the living room, use fabrics and furnishings that are slightly more formal than those in other areas of your home. Choose a deep sofa and cozy armchairs that are as comfortable as possible, so that the living room becomes a sought-after retreat for conversation and reading. Accessorize the room with special objects, but in keeping with today's lighter look, use them sparingly. Make sure there's a large ottoman or coffee table to hold a few refreshments when you entertain. Provide different kinds of lighting—wall sconces, table and floor lamps, shelf lights, and portrait lighting—so that you can adjust the level of illumination according to the time of day, the activity, and the mood. Here are some other options to consider.

• For a quick update, replace your old rug with one made of sisal or seagrass.

• Add soft pillows and beautiful throws to enhance the warm yet elegant feeling.

• Use plants, flowers, and scented candles to keep the room fresh; renew them frequently.

• Provide a source of music to enjoy while reading, relaxing, and entertaining.

Julia Hamilton
Senior Writer, *Southern Living*

Bold saffron walls belie this room's library-inspired design. **Traditional Charm:** From its built-in bookcases to the cozy fireplace, this is a room styled for comfort and function. The brass sconces mounted directly to the bookcase molding provide extra light. **Important Details:** A lively mix of colors and fabrics energizes this space. Yellow toile and blue-and-ivory silk fabrics give a nod to formality, while the patterned draperies and pillows add a casual attitude that keeps the room user-friendly. **Hidden Assets:** (inset) A secret closet in one of the bookcases is a clever space to stash books and magazines.

These two rooms provide proof that there's more than one way to approach decorating the living room. **Green's the Thing:** The bold citrus walls and ceiling set the stage for a fresh look that's enhanced by stark white trim and upholstery fabrics. A vinyl film applied to the glass panels in the built-ins' doors is an afford-able alternative to frosted glass. The film conceals bookshelves and helps hide clutter. **Add Ingredients and Mix Well:** Feel free to use an eclectic blend of accessories. This room features masks, art, and blue-and-white porcelain.

Natural fabrics and colors give a feeling of comfort without clutter. **Low Profile:** Placing low furniture in the center of the room preserves the openness of the space, which functions as a living and dining area. A draped sofa table separates the two areas of this room and also serves as a buffet. **Ivory Coats:** The dark gray wall of the bookcase contrasts well with the creamy accessories and books covered with off-white jackets. **French Twist:** Over the French doors, pewter swing-arm rods hold silk panels that are sewn from just two widths of cloth. They give the effect of full draperies that are open. (See larger photo on pages 8–9)

When living and dining areas are in one large space, establish a design common denominator. **Two for One:** Two neutral complementary colors are used on the walls in this two-story space to unify the living and dining areas and to bring the room to a more comfortable scale. Between the two colors, a scrolled stencil design, based on the dining room table's skirt fabric, spans both areas. **Not-So-Formal:** For the living room, two sofas set the color scheme of green and gold, with touches of red. A steel-and-glass console table visually separates the areas. Ottomans serve as a coffee table and provide extra seating. On each side of the fireplace, niches are filled with oversize mirrors and plants instead of the expected built-ins.

This room's combination of formal living and dining areas offers one generous, enjoyable space. **At Your Service:** In the dining room, two square plywood tables, skirted in tone-on-tone silk, are paired with rattan chairs (see photo at right). The tables can be pulled together to provide for more traditional dining or to serve as a casual buffet (above). A wall recess holds a hutch for displaying serving pieces.

"Accent the fireplace wall with accessories and art that are worthy of that important area." **Julia Hamilton**

Three pairs of French doors flood this living room with natural light, emphasizing its relaxed atmosphere. **Classic Lines:** A simple pediment above the mantel, made from coordinating molding, adds interesting detail and breaks up the expanse of the 24-foot-high wall. **Size Matters:** Large-scale furnishings match the lofty space. The tall armoire, grand sconces above the mantel, and lots of comfortable upholstered seating are a good fit and make the room feel more inviting.

The living room flows into the kitchen, so it's important that the colors make a smooth transition. **Free Association:** As the photos at left and above show, different fabric patterns in shades of moss green, wheat, and salmon give depth to the room's ambience. Aim for a balance of small, medium, and large patterns in similar hues for a successful mix. **More of the Same:** The gray-green finish on the kitchen island and the green wall on the back stairway just off the kitchen echo the colors in the living room and give a pleasing continuity to the entire area.

light & easy
family rooms

Family rooms are multitasking masters. We relax, eat, entertain, and sometimes even sleep in them—so comfort and versatility are key elements. In such a prominent room, you also want a big dose of personal style. Pulling all the ingredients together can be a challenge. To create a family room with flair, consider these tips.

• Everything doesn't have to match. Mixing wood finishes and including some iron and glass pieces gives a room more character.

• Consider two love seats instead of one sofa to break up a large room and provide more seating options.

• Look for pieces that do double duty, such as an ottoman that serves as a coffee table or a sofa table with a drop leaf that can be used as a buffet.

• Wear and tear is a concern in a room that's used so much. Make durable choices for upholstery, such as leather or chenille. For floors, a patterned rug is less likely to show stains.

• Pull out colors from a special painting or rug to help direct your color palette.

Alice Doyle
Homes Editor, *Southern Living*

Clever details make this family room, located at the heart of the house, a prime gathering spot.
Circle of Seats: Plentiful seating and stylishly comfortable furniture ensure that this room is enjoyed and well used. It's important that the seating arrangements be placed not too far apart, yet far enough that people can carry on private conversations. **Comfort and Ease:** The sofas are covered with neutral, textured fabrics that are easy to clean. **Table Matters:** An over-size coffee table accommodates large pillows underneath, allowing for casual dining.

"Enhance a neutral color palette by mixing textures and finishes, and tie it together with an eye-catching rug." **Alice Doyle**

Restful colors, rich upholstery fabrics, and plush furnishings beckon visitors into this study. **Have a Seat:** The seating in the room is functional for everyday use but can easily be rearranged to accommodate guests. The ottoman, normally used as a coffee table, can provide additional seating for a small gathering. A luxurious sofa and chair add comfort to the stylish room. **Aim High:** The curtains on one window go up to the molding to enhance the ceiling height and add a little drama. A decorative plaque above the French doors also draws attention to the tall ceiling.

This welcoming room is open yet intimate, with a mixture of formal and fun. **Shining Examples:** Lighting creates atmosphere. Include a mix of overhead lighting on dimmer switches, sconces, and lamps so you can easily change the mood. **Fabulous Furnishings:** The chenille fabric sofa and chairs furnish sink-in seating. Several antique tables add flair to the setting.

This family room is filled with displays of artwork mixed with favorite family heirlooms and travel souvenirs. **Focal Point:** Several elements highlight the fireplace, the centerpiece of the room. A tall log mantel flanked by a pair of chunky wood candlesticks complements the stone. An ornate iron piece beneath the mantel balances the dramatic drawing above. **Pattern Please:** The large and lively patterns of the club chairs, ottoman, and rug contrast nicely with the cream walls. **Accentuating Accessories:** Old pieces mix with newer ones to create a fresh style. Favorite paintings and collectibles fill the walls and tabletops.

The masculine character of this study mixes well with the comfortable seating. **Off the Wall:** Much of the lodgelike feel comes from the paneling and other millwork crafted of pecky cypress. **High Above:** The ceiling offers interest with a bright red tongue-and-groove paneled tray and an antler chandelier. **Mixture of Patterns and Textures:** The vibrant patterns of the rug and the draperies create a nice contrast with the more neutral club chairs and sofa.

A soaring ceiling, lots of windows, and tall mahogany doors make this beach house living room feel more spacious than it is. **Let the Outdoors In:** Tall, narrow windows make the porch feel like an extension of the room. Bright yellow rockers on the porch coordinate with the furniture inside. **Looking Good:** The seating area of the room is arranged in a horse-shoe to provide a great view from any angle. **Premium Blend:** Lightweight fabrics on the sofa, chair, and ottoman mix well with the wicker bench, whitewashed coffee table, and natural fiber rug.

Casual charm mixed with a hint of formality gives this room its distinction. **Looking Up:** Cedar beams used for the barrel-vault ceiling draw attention to the curved window. **Out of the Ordinary:** A painting hung on chain links against the backdrop of windows and draperies is an unexpected detail. **Keep It Interesting:** Various hard and soft materials throughout the room keep the color scheme from being dull. Iron, stone, leather, fabric, and wood fill the room with a pleasing mix of textures.

"Create a fresh seaside attitude with crisp colors, a splash of pattern, and a simple seagrass rug."

—Alice Doyle

open & airy
outdoor rooms

Today, homeowners are enjoying fully "decked-out" exterior spaces that can take whatever the elements dish out. With new developments in outdoor fabrics and related accessories, folks can treat outdoor features, such as porches, terraces, and decks, as they would interior spaces. Now when rain clouds appear on the horizon, there's no mad dash to drag everything inside! Here are some tips for making your outside space more livable.

• Look for furnishings specifically made for the outdoors and ones with breathable, quick-drying fabrics that can hold up to the relentless UV rays of the sun.

• Accessorize as you would your interior with pillows, plants, and other elements that can bear up to exposure to the weather.

• Instead of glass objects and tableware, use acrylic alternatives that won't break when tipped over by high winds.

• Make sure that any electrical items, such as lamps and stereo equipment, are plugged into outlets that are designed for outdoor use.

Rob Martin
Architecture Editor, *Southern Living*

Create a stylish outdoor living space by combining family room-style furniture and accessories with warm lighting. **New Look for Old Furniture:** Slipcovering furniture in a water-resistant fabric is a great way to get extra mileage out of it. Rust-resistant paint in a warm chocolate hue applied to the wrought-iron table and chairs protects them from outdoor elements. **Details Make the Difference:** Accessories give the look of a fully furnished family room. Plants in decorative pots lend a punch of color and function almost as draperies would in an interior room.

"Using furnishings fashioned from twigs, large vines, and other natural materials is a wonderful way to reflect your home's style and region." **Rob Martin**

The porches on this ranch hideaway suggest that outdoor spaces are as important as indoor ones. Sit a Spell: The back porch provides a good place to relax. It's a serene space that's perfect for reading or taking a nap in the hammock. **In the Mood:** Rustic twig furniture ensures an easy transition from the porch to the rest of the house. Piles of pillows—in tones of creams, browns, and reds—create soft seating. Potted plants add splashes of color, while hanging ferns create interest above. **Climate Control:** For hot summers, outdoor ceiling fans are a must for providing a cool breeze.

"A sisal rug is an excellent choice for a covered porch and a handsome complement to wicker furnishings."

Rob Martin

Porches, a Southern tradition, serve as extra rooms where homeowners can enjoy pleasant views and gentle breezes. **Furnished for Style and Function:** Rattan and wicker chairs can hold up to outdoor elements. The chairs shown here, cushioned in red, yellow, and green, create an attractive conversation area. **For the Floor:** A sisal rug defines the seating area and brings warmth and texture. **From the Top:** A copper-finish lantern contributes to the ambience. **Made for Shade:** This outdoor room respects porches of the past by using traditional shading devices, such as a trellis at one end.

"Ample entrances, such as these French doors, provide a visual connection to the exterior even when closed." **Rob Martin**

The casual attitude of this front porch invites neighbors to relax under the coolness of the ceiling fans and the deep shade created by the shed roof. **Curtain Call:** French doors flanked by dramatic window treatments connect the house and porch as one flowing space. **Simply Floored:** A stained-concrete floor scored in a tile pattern presents a rich touch of color and texture in combination with the stone walls. **Iron Art:** Iron accessories, such as the bench, tables, and screen, are a nice contrast to the stone on the porch.

This courtyard serves as an extension of the family room and draws guests into the garden. **Wall Flowers:** Limestone walls are juxtaposed with native landscape materials for a gentle contrast. **Spark of Interest:** The outdoor fireplace serves as a focal point of the courtyard and a natural gathering spot when the temperature drops. **Conversation Pieces:** Small furniture groupings create several intimate spaces for sitting and gathering.

For more on this kitchen, see page 51.

cooking &
dining spaces

pretty & practical
kitchens

Planning is essential in the kitchen. With a dizzying array of materials, colors, styles, and textures to choose from, the most popular room in the house can be one of the most fun and interesting to decorate. So even if it's just an easy update that you want and not a complete overhaul, consider these tips to set your plans in motion.

• Use rich, warm tones for a sophisticated and traditional look.

• To give the kitchen an expansive feel, paint cabinets a light color and select light-colored appliances.

• Bright colors juxtaposed against white cabinetry will instantly enlarge the look of a small kitchen.

• Neutral colors in a variety of textures of stone and tile create an inviting kitchen with interesting focal points.

• To add instant character, mix antique pieces with modern materials.

Tracy Sisson
Design Associate, *Southern Living At HOME*

Punctuated with color and antique and modern accents, this light and airy kitchen revolves around an ingenious island. **Moveable Feast:** This island is on casters and can be moved to make more room during parties or to simplify cleaning the floor. **No More Spills:** The island's stainless-steel top was custom designed with a lip around the edge to catch spills. **Splashes of Color:** Cherry wood crown molding, colorful Roman window shades, magenta cabinet interiors, and exotic houseplants spice up off-white walls. **Bright Ideas:** Lighting is abundant and beautiful with decorative antique pendants above the sink, efficient recessed cans in the ceiling, and task lighting under the cabinets.

"For appliances, use colors that recede into your decor, rather than shout for attention." **Tracy Sisson**

Elements of this updated 80-year-old kitchen downplay modern appliances in order to draw attention to the natural beauty of its marble countertops and unique decorative touches. **Great Cover-up:** Modern appliances don't distract from the vintage spirit, thanks to false cabinet fronts. Especially clever is the cabinet and drawer false front on the dishwasher (see insets). **Mad for Marble:** Marble is softer and more susceptible to staining than other surface materials, but if you love the depth and swirl of its character, stone sealers can help provide protection. The patina of age just adds to its beauty. **Cottage Classic:** Based on old pie chests, circular cutouts backed with cane embellish the upper cabinets. **Personality Plus:** Above the sink are a stylish stainless steel clock and a shelf displaying a collection of glass cake stands; on the window ledge is an ivy-filled urn. Mirrors on the backsplash and an antique shaving mirror mounted on a heavy swivel frame above the cooktop work like windows to open up the room.

This kitchen in a historic home unites old-world detail with sleek modern amenities. **The Big Island:** This large island, painted a color from the tile backsplash and topped with butcher block, houses a sink and adds abundant storage. It also serves as a breakfast bar for the family and a buffet for entertaining. **Featured Attraction:** The built-in hutch in an earthy gray rivals the stainless-steel range and hood for attention. Favorite things are showcased in glass-front cabinets and on open shelves. **At Hand:** Strategically placed shelves over the range and beside the hutch provide out-of-the-way access for ingredients and accessories.

A refreshing face-lift transforms this not-so-new, not-so-big kitchen. **Cabinet Cosmetics:** Painting or restaining existing cabinets in light shades makes the whole room seem larger, as does adding glass cabinet fronts. Add stock trim molding to flat-front cabinets for a change of style. **Almost Instant Update:** Today's selection of cabinet knobs and pulls seems endless. Replace hardware for a quick and easy new look. **Up and Away:** A built-in plate shelf, a microwave shelf, and a hanging rack for pots and pans are space-saving storage solutions.

"To contrast the cabinetry, incorporate different colors, styles, and types of materials for built-in storage pieces." Tracy Sisson

"Mixing a variety of textures in stone and tile creates a sophisticated kitchen with interesting focal points." **Tracy Sisson**

Earthy texture abounds from floor to ceiling in this rustic kitchen. **Leading Role:** Wood is the star in this kitchen but is never typecast. It makes appearances as a beaded-board ceiling, wide-plank floors, cabinets stained a muted gray-brown, a generous trestle table, and bar-stools. **Complementary Cast:** Stone back-splashes, tin countertops, and punched-tin panels in the pantry door add a rich background texture. Old-fashioned crates underneath the island and spatterware hanging from the over-head rack suit the cabinlike quality.

A Light Touch: Open-backed, glass-front upper cabinets mounted to the windows let in light. Colorful plates and glasses displayed in the space reflect rainbow patterns as the sun hits them—a fun effect in this casual setting.

This kitchen blurs the line between living spaces by employing accents from other rooms. **Kitchen Comforts:** Artwork, upholstered seating, rugs, and decorative fabric treatments soften utilitarian aspects of this kitchen and make it a popular gathering spot. Vintage tole trays on the wall and a copper lamp on the countertop make the kitchen as well appointed as any room in the house.

"To make the kitchen more welcoming, mix antiques with modern materials." Tracy Sisson

A Room That's in View: Because the breakfast table in this kitchen is visible from the front door, it's covered with a floor-length skirt and square table topper in richly patterned fabrics that complement the living room decor.

"Fabric introduces a cozy mood by softening hard lines and edges of windows." **Tracy Sisson**

Sumptuous seating invites lingering meals in a sunny corner of this kitchen. **Built-in Beauty:** An L-shaped banquette is tucked under spacious windows and plumped with pillows in coordinating fabrics. **Featured Fashions:** A generous valance, a table lamp, and a painting accent the small space with decorative details.

This welcoming kitchen is the heart of the home, providing a comfortable area for the family to cook, dine, and relax. **Generous Scale:** This grand space features tall ceilings, expansive counter space, creamy cabinetry with rich crown molding, dramatic granite back-splashes, tile floors, and abundant eat-in options. **Ample Seating:** The mixed wood finishes of the island barstools, the dining table, and the Windsor chairs add a casual contrast. A bench against the wall beckons invitingly. Botanical prints above the bench and color-coordinated cushions are soft, serene touches. (See larger photo on pages 38–39.)

big ideas for
breakfast
rooms

For many families, the need to maximize space in the home is high on the priority list. So creating a dining area that performs more than one duty is a good solution. A well-designed breakfast area is not only perfect for the morning cereal ritual, but also can be a great place to do homework or share a cup of tea with a neighbor. It should be as comfortable and inviting as the living room, with the same convenience and efficiency as the rest of the kitchen. Here are some ideas to help you turn your breakfast area into your favorite spot in the house.

• Use fabric to spice up chairs and a table. Cushions for seating and maybe a colorful tablecloth will add spark to an ordinary dining area.

• Provide color and flair with simple window fashions. Valances and shades make great top-of-the-window treatments when space is limited.

• Create a casual seating element by using a couple of upholstered chairs in conjunction with standard dining chairs.

Sarah Jernigan
Interior Design Coordinator, *Southern Living*

A table and chairs in matching wood tones, fabric seat covers, and a rug give this breakfast room its own identity. **Island Attraction:** A work island creates a distinct divide between the kitchen and breakfast room. The island's creamy painted finish strikes a pleasing contrast with the pecan brown of the dining table and chairs, and reinforces the separation between the areas. The wood finishes, including the stained ceiling, enrich the rooms with warm overtones. **Clearly Interesting:** Glass-front cabinet doors are an engaging way to establish depth. The stone wall, the deep green tile backsplash, and the black shutters at the kitchen window add vitality to the decorating scheme.

"A banquette, or built-in booth-style seating, maximizes seating in a narrow area or tight corner." **Sarah Jernigan**

Consider built-in or freestanding benches instead of chairs as a good seating solution for a narrow space. **Cozy Corners:** Banquette seating, anchored by a rectangular table, makes the most of this breakfast room's space. Additional chairs complement the permanent seating and add flexibility. They can be moved to another room to allow more walking space in the breakfast area. **Fill in the Details:** Richly patterned fabrics used on the banquette and throw pillows give this setting its inviting ambience. Linen café curtains hanging from iron rods add privacy and a soft accent at the windows. **Style and Substance:** A casual, decorative chandelier provides ample light and visually fills the space between the dining table and the high ceiling.

Shades of red weave throughout this room's design, creating a visually exciting harmony. **Intriguing Array:** Bold and subtle patterns add punch to the unconventional combination of wing chairs, an upholstered settee, and slipcovered wooden chairs. The rug under the table carries the color theme and draws the furnishings together. **Tops in Style:** A fringed valance loops over painted drapery finials attached to the wall. The quilted valance is accented with pleats lined with red check fabric, adding another eye-catching pattern to the mix.

Warm colors and textures give this open-plan breakfast room an intimate ambience.
Natural Charm: Woven rattan dining chairs and a sisal rug create a distinct sense of space in a breakfast area that is situated in a generously sized open area between the living room and the kitchen. **Tall, Dark, and Handsome:** A freestanding, deep red storage piece is a cornerstone of the furniture arrangement. The hutch and wooden farmhouse table convey a European country look that echoes the decorating theme of the rest of the house.

The caramel tone of the kitchen cabinets continues the color scheme and enhances the flow between spaces. **Gold Standard:** Sunnyhued walls, maple cabinets, and red-and-gold valances at the windows unify and support the design motif across three different living areas: the kitchen, breakfast room, and living room. Common colors and textures play an important role in a large, open arrangement by creating a smooth transition from one space to the next.

Shades of taupe and green and a scattering of earthy fabrics and accessories make a soothing setting for starting the day. **A Natural Choice:** Fern print wallpaper (which also covers the ceiling) and acorn wood carvings continue the botanical theme that also shows itself in the floral rug, accent pillows on the built-in banquette, and the wicker dining chairs. Remnant fabrics are a good source for making pillows, which add color to the setting. **On Display:** The neutral palette here is an excellent backdrop for a collection of transferware. Displaying collections personalizes a room. For a more dramatic impact, group small accessories instead of separating them.

"Mixing upholstered pieces with wood and adding decorative elements on the wall give the room a fresh personality."

Sarah Jernigan

A drop-leaf table is a clever space-saving choice for a small dining area. **Building Character:** Even in a tiny room, accessories can make the difference between a ho-hum decor and one with lots of zing. Here, the colors from the lively plaid on the chairs inspire the selection of accent pieces, such as the golden votive holders and the amber-toned bottles holding yellow zinnias. **Added Extras:** Woven baskets on top of the storage unit, the multidimensioned frame on the mirror, and the richly textured lampshade are key ingredients in forming this room's inviting mood.

delightful designs for
dining rooms

Dining rooms have evolved from formal and traditional to comfortable and unique spaces. Sitting down to share a meal with friends and family is such an expression of love and appreciation that the room you share this time in should reflect your personal style. Consider these ideas when furnishing your dining room.

• Take your time as you begin collecting pieces to furnish your dining room. Choose items that you love. You want to appreciate them more in a decade than you do the day you purchase them.

• After you have selected the furniture, start adding texture to your dining space with rugs and fabrics.

• When selecting a rug, make sure all your chairs fit on the rug when they're pulled away from the table; otherwise, it can mean damage to hardwoods and frustration as you try to sit down to and get up from the table.

• To refresh the decorating scheme in the dining room, reupholster or slipcover the seats of your chairs.

Melanie Grant
Director of Design, *Southern Living At HOME*

Like many traditional dining rooms, this space has a formal edge but feels more casually elegant than stiff and uncomfortable. **In the Mood:** Stylish doesn't have to mean stuffy. Ivory fabrics on the chairs and dark wood pair for an upscale feel that is tempered by an earthy sisal rug and draperies hung from metal rods. Even the bold check on the drapery border contributes to the dressed-up yet laid-back feeling. **Versatile White:** White china offers a lot of table-setting options. It contrasts well with the dark wood of the table and makes a good backdrop for the blue-and-white accents in the china cabinet. The centerpiece, comprised of a vase in a compote, adds height to the table.

A stately fireplace and mantel set a formal tone in this dining room. The ornate chandelier and minimal accessories contribute to the dressy mood. **Room to Grow:** A dining table with removable leaves is a flexible choice for entertaining in a formal setting, allowing the table to accommodate any number of guests. **Window Dressing:** In a room that features mainly wooden furnishings, such as a dining room, window treatments are key to softening the look. Choosing a simple-patterned or neutral fabric that will complement a variety of decorating styles is a smart move, since the investment in draperies often means they're in use for many years.

When planning a new dining room, remember that details, such as a wainscot with raised panels and elaborate crown molding, add depth. **Hip to Be Square:** A skirted round dining table provides a pleasing contrast in this square room. A basic table form covered with a dressy silk tablecloth is an economical alternative to a traditional table. This simplicity is balanced by elegant dining chairs.

This room's design starts with beautiful striped silk fabric for the windows. From there, the other colors and patterns fall into place. **A Tuck Here, a Nip There:** Existing chairs get a face-lift with slipcovers—a less pricey option than buying new chairs. Here, a blue print is used for the Chippendale-style chairs and a bright yellow linen covers the slipper chairs. Both fabrics complement the window panels. **Casual Attire Okay:** A patterned sisal rug keeps the room from looking too formal. The texture of the rug contrasts nicely with the silk draperies, elegant chandelier, and French commode that does double duty as a buffet (see photo below).

Consider a multipurpose piece that can hold linens and also serve as a buffet. **Custom Creation:** A French reproduction chest doubles as a buffet when needed. The ornate mirror and lamps round out the vignette. When hanging a mirror, be sure the reflection is something other than a blank wall. Here, the reflection of the painted screen adds an engaging dimension to the room. **Light Effects:** Table lamps cast a warm glow in the dining room and help illuminate areas not covered by the overhead chandelier. For instant ambience, install dimmer switches on overhead fixtures.

"This fabulous screen adds color and interest, and gives the room a refined personality." **Melanie Grant**

Matching drapery fabric and wallpaper create a cozy softness while making a big design impact.
Double the Fun: A toile design with cream-and-green tones dresses the windows and walls. Though
the pattern is busy, the color scheme and the repetition of the design provide a surprisingly neutral
backdrop. A screen with a chinoiserie theme makes the room more intimate, and an Oriental rug adds
color. **Fashion Extras:** The table is draped in a pleated chenille cloth with tasseled fringe for a tailored
look that is an attractive counterpoint to the toile. Thick chair-rail molding and beaded-board wainscot
details give the room a cottage look.

"A Southwestern influence, expressed in rich colors and textures, gives this space its unique allure." **Melanie Grant**

A real-life ranch house is steeped in authentic Western-style tradition. **Gather 'Round:** A wooden farm table is the star feature in this dining space. A bench and handcrafted upholstered wooden chairs offer flexible seating. Stacked-up foldable chairs in the corner of the room are easily pressed into service for unexpected guests. **All for One:** Every detail enhances the common theme. Western art on the wall, rustic iron candleholders on the table, and a chandelier complete with leather-laced shades are on-target accents for the log walls and ceiling. A woven rug in shades of red, cream, and woodsy brown adds a punch of bright color and pattern.

"Fresh flowers and candles are quick ways to dress the dining room for a party." Melanie Grant

Wood tones in the dining room should complement each other in color and texture. **Dark Impact:** The black wood frame of the mirror is an exclamation point of color against the honey-hued table and display cabinet, and keeps the furnishings from looking too much like a matched set. **Everything Old Is New Again:** Slipcovers give new life to tired furnishings. They're also an easy way to change the look to match the season.

"A mix of casual and elegant elements makes for an inviting room that people aren't afraid to use." Melanie Grant

Neutral upholstery, such as the creamy damask used for the dining room chairs, is the accent of choice in a room with a bold wall color. **A Question of Balance:** Creating a comfortable dining room that still heralds a distinct character is all in the mix. Here, an iron table with a painted wooden top and two styles of chairs set the tone for a lively blend. Damask slipcovers on the Queen Anne–style chairs convey a formal attitude, but the cotton finish makes them more relaxed. Slipcovers add softness to a dining room, which typically has a lot of hard surfaces. **Simpatico Style:** Combining two types of chairs in the dining room adds visual interest, especially if you have a lot of them.

bedroom retreats

For more on this bedroom, see page 79.

easy & elegant bedrooms

The sole purpose of the bedroom is to be peaceful and accommodating. With that in mind, furnish it with elements that you find soothing. Are they things from the woods, the sea, the garden? Once you've decided on the source of inspiration for your room, decorating is a piece of cake.

• Keep the bed as the focal point of the room. If possible, place it on a far wall, away from the doorway. Area rugs add comfort and warmth.

• If you must include a work space or television in the bedroom, consider using a screen or armoire that can separate these areas from the rest of the room.

• Use aromatherapy in the bedroom. A scented candle or fragrant flowers by the side of the bed encourages a restful mood.

• Consider how light affects the room. If the room is sunny, line window treatments to help block the morning sun.

Rose Nguyen
Photo Stylist, *Southern Living*

Soft and conservative, this master bedroom is a sophisticated retreat. **Neutral Base:** Pale taupe walls and neutral flooring allow other elements to take center stage. Delicate floral curtains and bedcovers introduce color with soothing pinks and greens. The bed, with its rich-hued wood and diamond design, adds the drama. **Not-So-Plain Geometry:** Geometrical patterns—the design on the bed frame and the plaid print on the chair—balance the floral theme echoed in the bedding, curtains, and framed botanicals. **Mix and Match:** Feel free to use a variety of complementary styles in a room. Here, mismatched tables and bedside lamps add character.

"Layering different textures of the same mono-chromatic scheme is an effective way to bring elegance into your bedroom." **Rose Nguyen**

Aqua-and-taupe bed linens inspire this bedroom's overall scheme. **Tailored to Perfection:** A simple linen bedskirt and an Ultrasuede-covered headboard complement the elegant duvet and shams. Decorative upholstery tacks on the headboard finish off this tailored look. **Grand Proportions:** A high headboard and a frame that elevates the mattress 18 inches keep the width of this king-size bed in proportion. Other pieces relate well to the bed's scale: Bedside tables match the height of the mattress; elongated lamps reach up to the top of the headboard, a good height for reading.

The window seat, framed by built-in bookcases, defines the sitting area. **Functional Beauty:** The window seat and elevated bed yield ample storage beneath. The lower half of the bookcase on the right opens up and serves as a desk. A comfortable chair nearby stands ready as a practical accent piece. **An Eclectic Mix:** Favorite items accessorize the bedroom and give it personal flair.

Achieve richness with subtle colors and tone-on-tone texture. **Distinguished Taste:** A plantation bed dressed in luxurious fabrics—along with fringed curtains, an oil painting, and heavy lamps—creates a sense of weight and importance. Soft greens and creamy yellows keep the room light and relaxing. **Dramatic Symmetry:** The plantation bed makes a strong statement. Centering it between the two windows keeps the room in balance. **Personal Details:** An array of frames in various shapes, sizes, and colors showcases family pictures. Vases filled with flowers add an elegant touch.

Dreamy silvery greens set the tone for this haven of sleep. **Serene Scene:** From the barely-there wall color to the deep olive accents on the duvet, the shades of green provide contrast and depth in a soothing setting. **Sense of Touch:** Velvets, chenilles, and silks add textural softness and variety. **Celestial Aspirations:** Curtains hung at the ceiling and wrought-iron bedposts reaching skyward make the walls seem to extend into infinity.

"Use architectural elements to add interest and texture. Flea markets are a good source for inexpensive finds. Garden gates or vintage shutters or doors can be easily mounted on the wall as a beautiful alternative to a headboard." **Rose Nguyen**

European artwork, an antique secretary, and an Oriental rug lend old-world flair to this room. **Room with a View:** The grand window brings the outside in and inspires the room's design theme. Potted plants and a wrought-iron headboard, reminiscent of a garden gate, maintain the open-air feel. Using low furnishings, such as the desk and ottoman, keeps the focus on the view. **Fine Treatment:** Fabric treatments for arched windows can be challenging. Here, straight rods above the side windows and knobs above the curved window hold the chenille draperies in place. **Invitation to Indulge:** If possible, include a bench or chair in the bedroom arrangement. Add soft throw pillows to create a comfortable spot to relax.

Bring a fresh color scheme full circle. **Golden Palette:** The honey tones of the solid wood bed are repeated in the yellow-gold walls and fabrics. The painted dresser and nightstand add artistic detail to the monochromatic scheme, as do the golden framed mirror, antique plates over the bed, and pine serving tray. A large coordinating area rug draws all the elements together. **Private Matters:** Plantation shutters provide privacy; fabric panels and painted valances soften the lines. (See larger photo on pages 70–71.)

In shades of blue and green, this bedroom defines femininity. **Coordinating Patterns:** Flower-stenciled walls and green gingham curtains add a simple charm. A vintage-inspired fabric graces the bedspreads and valances. Twin beds with upholstered head- and footboards feature a scallop print. When mixing patterns, pay attention to the scale of the designs. Use only one large pattern, such as the valance and duvet fabric shown here. Complement it with designs in similar colors but with smaller patterns, such as the wallpaper and the upholstery fabric on the beds. **Mirror Image:** Dishes displayed on a plate rack reflect the leafy patterns on the bedspreads, walls, and valances. **Color Punch:** Round red-and-gold pillows borrow accent colors from the fabrics and add a playful brightness.

Lavender toile–covered walls and a bright white floor and ceiling set a sunny tone. **Color Works:** Toile bedding, sheer white curtains, and a white iron crib give this room a crisp yet inviting decor. **Shades of White:** An antique finish and gold accents on the bed and nightstands soften the look. Pale furnishings often allow for more flexibility in the choice of fabric colors. **For Baby:** Polka-dot rugs and a bunny chandelier with gingham shades keep this nursery with a guest bed child-friendly.

"Choose classic furniture and a simple color scheme that can grow with your children. Rely on accessories to update the look as they get older." **Rose Nguyen**

Filled with fairies and fanciful bugs, this girl's room sets the imagination free. **Child's Play:** A soothing two-tone paint treatment in lavender and green is the setting for this fantastical room; fabrics, toys, and accessories, such as whimsical butterfly- and heart-shaped pillows, bring it to life. **Fancy Free:** White furniture interjects a cool simplicity into this otherwise animated space. A painted armoire complements the walls. **Art for All Ages:** By hanging one of the framed fairy prints on the lower half of the wall, the art is at a child's eye level while enjoyable to all.

Add color and whimsy by attaching ribbons to sheer curtain panels. **Fairyland Frills:** The magical theme continues with fairies embroidered on sheer curtains hung from a white wrought-iron trellis-style valance. Satin ribbon bows in coordinating colors are tied to the valance, which is attached directly to the ceiling. This idea can be easily adapted for an ordinary rod by tacking or pinning bows where the top of plain curtain panels attach to the rod.

For more on this detail, see page 95.

decorating details

creative
wall
arrangements

You can make a powerful decorating
statement with wall arrangements.
The secret is all in the presentation.
Start by considering your favorite collections of framed prints or pieces of art.
Mixing is okay. Contemporary pieces can
work well with traditional ones; gold
frames can work with silver ones. Blend
textures, such as wrought iron with antique
porcelain. To achieve a balanced look,
arrange smaller pieces on the top and bottom, and hang heavier pieces in the center.
Here are a few basics to keep in mind.

• Arrange your collections on the floor
first before hanging them on the wall. This
way you can move pieces around easily
without damaging your walls.

• Create drama by making interesting
shapes when grouping arrangements.

• Go beyond framed art or decorative
plates. With the
proper hardware
and tools, you can
hang just about
anything.

Mary Leigh Fitts
Assistant Projects Editor, *Southern Living*

A sure bet for a wall arrangement that works is for the various elements to share a common theme. **Horse Show:** Prints and paintings depicting horses hang in a symmetrical arrangement. The desk offers a logical starting point for positioning the grouping, which is centered above the desktop. Hanging the heavier paintings in the middle gives good visual balance. **Not to Be Forgotten:** Man's best friend finds a place among the racing crowd. Though the sketch of the dog differs in subject from the other framed pieces, the coloring and character of the print and frame make it a suitable complement.

The dimensional character of ironwork is visually intriguing. Compared to traditional art, it shows line and shadow instead of color and imagery. **Compatible Composition:** Two pieces of fan-shaped ironwork mounted above a plaster-relief shelf introduce different materials to the already eclectic mix of furniture, fabrics, plants, and collectibles in the room. **Hang in There:** Be sure to hang ironwork from bolts or nails—preferably inserted into wall studs—that are sturdy enough to provide adequate support.

"The theme of a wall grouping can set the tone for the entire room." **Mary Leigh Fitts**

A collection of prints uniformly framed and hung has the impact of a museum-size piece at a fraction of the cost. **Gridlock:** All these botanical prints came from one old book. Each page is simply matted and placed in a green-stained oak frame. In this setting, the gridlike placement of the prints is key to the grouping's success—it reads like one unit instead of a dozen different parts. **Garden Works:** The outdoorsy fern illustrations carry out the nature theme seen in other accessories in the room, such as the antique beehive atop the pie safe in the corner and the bee motif on the pillows.

"Look for art in unexpected places. Plates are prime examples of multi-purpose pieces that are both practical and decorative." **Mary Leigh Fitts**

Be bold in your selection of wall decorations. Often the most utilitarian pieces make impressively graceful transformations. Set for Change: A handsome iron plate rack is priceless when it comes to changeable art displays. Here, plates are featured, but the rack could hold small framed prints instead. The look can reflect the season or the mood. **Close Companion:** Be sure that the decoration doesn't look lost on the wall. Placing this narrow piece alongside a window with a rich drapery panel anchors it and gives it more visual presence.

Decorate with what you love without spending a fortune. Make your collections great conversation pieces by grouping them. **Power in Numbers:** A good rule of thumb is that items make a grander appearance when displayed together. Resist the temptation to spread them across the room just to cover more square footage. **Shape Up:** Here, seven transferware plates are hung from wire plate hangers and arranged in a triangle above the bookcase. A teapot resting on a stack of books is another beloved collectible.

showcasing
collections

Using favorite objects to decorate your home places your personal signature on your surroundings and shares your interests with friends and family. It's also the best way to fill your rooms with the things you love. Any room can benefit from an artfully arranged grouping. Consider these suggestions when displaying your treasures.

• Stagger heights for visual interest. Use a mix of short and tall pieces, or place small bowls or statues on a stack of books to elevate them.

• Choose accessories with a common color for a unified look.

• Vary textures to give an interesting contrast. For example, accentuate the surface of a rusty iron object by placing it alongside a glazed porcelain piece.

• Change your displays frequently. Rotate items, keeping some in storage while placing others on view.

Lisa Powell
Assistant Photo Stylist, *Southern Living*

To emphasize a collection, gather items of similar color. **Warm Tones:** A platter, plates, and a metal tray, all in shades of gold, form an impressive arrangement because they share a common color theme. Black iron candle sconces frame the grouping and add interesting detail. **Plant Power:** When possible, integrate fresh flowers and plants into the setting. Here, tall olive jars holding branches of bittersweet and mums merge seamlessly with the wall decorations.

A collection of majolica dishes decorates a cupboard and wall, establishing a botanical motif in the room. **Shared Identity:** Use a collection to strengthen a decorating scheme. The pottery's garden theme spills over to other elements of the room, such as the bamboo shades on the French doors and the botanical print fabric on the chairs. **No Boundaries:** This collection works on multiple surfaces. Here, pottery plates grace the wall and fill the cupboard. Additional majolica pieces, such as pitchers and vases, fill in among the plates. **Plan Ahead:** For a wall grouping, arrange the plates on the floor first; then when you find a configuration that pleases you, hang the plates on the wall.

Any gathering of similar objects can form a collection. **Easy Does It:** Something as simple as candles in your favorite colors becomes a decorating statement when artfully arranged. **Common Ground:** Pears and delicate branches of leaves punch up the presence of the pillar candles. Use a large platter or tray to unify small items for more impact. (See larger photo on pages 84–85.)

"*Favorite art and collections personalize a room.*" **Lisa Powell**

Harmonizing diverse objects in a space involves some experimentation. **Artful Alliance:** To achieve the appealing look of well-filled shelves, begin by placing the larger objects. Fill in with smaller ones, leaving open spaces for artwork and favorite accessories. Add these pieces last, and continue rearranging them until you strike a pleasing balance. **Tools of the Trade:** Use plate stands, small boxes, and books to give prominence to various small items. To enliven the space, include fresh elements, such as plants, fruits, and flowers.

Arranging several small items together creates a more dramatic presentation. **A Charming Trio:** Use everyday objects in groups to make a design statement. For a buffet, three vases form a pleasing and practical vignette. **Perfect Positioning:** Give intricately detailed objects, such as these candle-holders, special emphasis by placing them against a simple background. **Group Effort:** Mass a collection of framed photographs to give them greater impact. Stagger the placement so each is visible. **Reaching New Heights:** Stacking small objects is a good way to increase their importance as decorative elements. Three small paintings hanging together as a unit make a stronger statement than just one.

focus on the
fireplace

A fireplace is a guaranteed attention-getter in a room. Since most fireplaces have either a mantel or a hearth—or both—they offer the perfect stage for creative decorating. These ideas will make the fireplace and mantel an ever-changing venue for displays to suit your mood, the seasons, or special occasions.

• For a classic look, keep mantel accessories in symmetrical balance; for example, place one candlestick or vase at each end of the mantel. An asymmetrical arrangement often conveys a more casual attitude.

• The wall above the fireplace can be an area of major interest and a good spot to display a distinctive, one-of-a-kind accessory.

• Use unusual objects for imaginative vignettes. Old architectural fragments, small garden statues, shell collections, even teacups and saucers are suitable decorations for the mantel.

• Plants are a lively addition to the fireplace area. Place topiaries in urns, or line the mantel with a row of simple vases or jars filled with fresh blooms.

Cari South
Assistant Photo Stylist, *Southern Living*

Consider the style of the fireplace and the surrounding accessories when planning a mantel decoration. **A Little Romance:** Picking up a flowery theme from the ornate scrollwork on the fireplace and mirror frame is the key to making a simple line of candles a stunning showpiece. Tiny blooms tucked among the pillars are a fitting finishing touch. **Double Image:** Mirrors possess phenomenal power to multiply the dramatic impact of an arrangement. The warm glow of candlelight creates an especially effective reflection.

"Rethink the ordinary when planning your fireplace decoration. Flea markets and salvage shops are good places to spark creative flair." **Cari South**

Look past an object's original use to envision a new purpose for it. **Creative Karma:** A weathered metal gate rescued from a salvage yard has new life as a screen for the fireplace. Above the mantel, an arched window frame surrounds tiny pots of dried blooms hanging on the wall. **Odds and Ends:** The intricate mantel, complete with little ledges that are perfect for books, is topped with glazed pots filled with branches and flowers, fresh fruits in a wooden bowl, and a vintage finial. Wicker-wrapped jugs and a lamp made from an old wooden column add interesting character to the scene.

You can create a mantel decoration any time of year, not just for Christmas. **Point of Interest:** Let the mantel be an everchanging stage for fresh displays. Candleholders and olive jars are the framework of this display. Lacy branches, fruits, nuts, and flowers add color and rich texture. **Companion Pieces:** The colors on the mantel work in perfect harmony with the artwork hanging above.

Keep the hearth in mind when decorating your fireplace. **Think Fresh:** A deep red stool and bright berry stems give a shot of color to this stone hearth. The stool elevates the urn and positions it at a better height to be noticed. **Defining Details:** Add utilitarian items with an eye to design. Basic necessities, such as fire tools and a screen, can also function as attractive accents.

"Since the fireplace commands such attention in the room, use that space to display favorite collectibles as well." Cari South

Set a cozy scene around the fireplace with comfortable seating, books, and treasured accessories in abundance. Old-world Charm: A distinctive fireplace can dictate the mood of the room. This rustic stone fireplace evokes an English country feel. **It's All in the Details:** Staffordshire statues on shelves, a favorite pet's portrait in a place of honor, and accents—such as the iron fireplace tools, match holder, and hand-painted fire blower—reinforce the theme.

In some settings, the best decorating skill to possess is restraint. **Structurally Sound:** When the fireplace itself is a work of art, there's little need to embellish it. Minimal accessorizing allows the texture and color of the limestone to be the featured attraction. **Natural Materials:** A plant arrangement with leggy willow accents on the coffee table and a spiky plant against the wall add color and texture.

grace notes

For more on this tablescape, see page 109.

simply charming
tablescapes

The way you set a table is a reflection of your personal style. Whether it's formal, casual, contemporary, whimsical, or a combination of looks, you'll find that anything goes as long as you follow a few easy guidelines.

• It's okay to mix and match. Choose flatware, dishes, and glasses that coordinate but don't necessarily match to create a unique look.

• Keep it simple. Focus on one or two predominant colors for your table and accentuate in varying shades.

• Almost anything can be a centerpiece. Look for ideas among your favorite collections of baskets, vases, or pots.

• Combine vivid colors and rich textures for maximum impact.

• Flowers and greenery are key ingredients to introducing a beautiful mood to any setting.

Buffy Hargett
Senior Photo Stylist, *Southern Living*

Fresh fruits and flowers create an inviting atmosphere for an outdoor Southern luncheon.
Pineapple Bowls: Pineapple halves make unique serving dishes for a colorful array of fresh fruits. Miniature pineapples encircled with roses sit inside tiny urns and repeat the fruity theme. **Stand Tall:** A cake stand elevates an arrangement of flowers and grapes covered by a wire conservatory. **On the Side:** To avoid overcrowding the table, additional food and beverages are placed on a side table. An assortment of iron baskets and trays serves a variety of purposes in this table setting—as elegant containers for appetizers, as trays for drinks, and especially as decoration.

*"Natural materials
enliven this setting.
Pears, a smattering of
nuts, and green apples
add impact."* **Buffy Hargett**

The soft glow of candlelight illuminates a mix of vibrant flowers, berries, and fruits. **Center Stage:** Bright red amaryllis provide a brilliant burst of color among bunches of grapes and berries in a moss-lined iron container. **Party Lights:** Candlelight, in the form of twisted tapers, pillars, and votives, contributes to the cheery mood. To make the green apple votive holders, carve out the tops of the apples just enough to hold small votive candles. Tuck in tiny bits of moss around the candles, well below the wicks. **Metal Works:** Copper-hued chargers placed under pottery dinner plates add a graceful finish to the table setting.

Count on candles to say special occasion. **Light Touch:** Candles floating in water-filled vases form a fast centerpiece that sacrifices nothing when it comes to elegant impact. **Main Attraction:** A beautiful bowl of white blooms appears to reflect the soft glow of the candle-light. (See larger photo on pages 104–105.)

"Serving pieces in a variety of heights and sizes add punch to this simple setting."

Buffy Hargett

Re-create an outdoor setting reminiscent of the old-fashioned Sunday dinners that are the essence of Southern style and hospitality. **Short Stack:** A tiered plate stand adds height to the table decoration and offers an attractive means of placing food on the table. **Season's Best:** Cutting flowers and greenery from the garden is an inexpensive way to dress the table in native beauty. Here, hydrangeas and magnolias go straight from the garden to the table. **Awash in White:** All the serving platters—even the centerpiece urn—are white, making a crisp look that shows off the colorful food.

"This centerpiece draws its impact from the repetition of green glass and fresh flowers." **Buffy Hargett**

The beauty of a well-prepared table lies in the details. **Start with the Basics:** Create an inviting table setting with a few everyday items. For example, these clear glass jars serve as great centerpiece containers. **Generous Clippings:** Flowers lend a seasonal fragrance to the surroundings. They are luscious arranged in the center of the table and then repeated as napkin-ring accents. **Location, Location, Location:** Dining beneath the shade of a large tree leaves little to be desired—though comfy, cushioned wicker chairs and crisp table linens certainly contribute to the luxurious feeling.

The daisy design on the tablecloth sets the tone of this garden get-together. Springlike colors are in every detail—from the cupcakes to the party favors. **Rickrack Rules:** A big square of fabric trimmed with jumbo rickrack makes a fine table topper over a colorful swath of burlap. **Daisy Decorations:** Gerbera daisies bring touches of whimsy to the chair backs and take center stage arranged on a floral foam ball at the center of the table. A cake stand is the perfect pedestal for the floral orb. **Special Favors:** Memo pads embellished with felt daisies are fun party favors in keeping with the floral theme.

Candlelight sets a shimmering tablescape. **Easy Math:** Multiply the dramatic effect by grouping hurricane vases in varied sizes to create an interesting display. Mixing the candle colors gives a casual air.

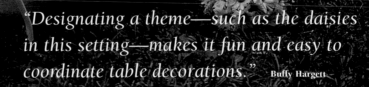

"Designating a theme—such as the daisies in this setting—makes it fun and easy to coordinate table decorations." **Buffy Hargett**

fun with *flowers*

Flowers brighten any day, make us feel special, and give us beauty, color, and fragrance. Using flowers in the home is the simplest way to change the mood, and color is one of the most important elements. Yellow and red blooms are happy and bright. White and green flowers are calming and soothing. When it comes to working with flowers, have fun and incorporate some of these ideas.

• Be creative when selecting containers. Pitchers, teacups, and drinking glasses make ideal vases. Also consider baskets, urns, and bowls. If necessary, create the arrangement in a waterproof container, and then set it inside the decorative one.

• An easy way to style cut flowers is to first arrange the stems in your hand, and then place the entire bouquet in the vase.

• To hide stems, fill large, clear vases with fruits, shells, or other objects before adding water.

• Mix fruits and vegetables with flowers to add a unique, colorful element to the display.

Kay Clarke
Senior Photo Stylist, Oxmoor House

Chrysanthemums are fall's flowers. Bring the season indoors with inexhaustible blooms.
Easily Contained: This hearty arrangement is housed in an old-fashioned chicken feeder filled with floral foam. **One-Stop Shopping:** All these materials can be purchased while grocery shopping. Start with large pompon football mums and a bunch or two of smaller blooms in complementary tones. From the produce section, bring home heads of colorful kale and selections of persimmons, pomegranates, lady apples, and artichokes. To make arranging simple and to avoid a structured look, use odd numbers of items.

The graceful curve of tulip stems adds to the beauty of their arrangement. **Container Magic:** The top of this vase has holes in it—similar to a floral frog—that guide the placement of the flowers and anchor them in the vase. The container gets additional height from a decorative cake stand. **Tulip Tips:** Before arranging tulips, remove the firm white portions at the bottoms of the stems. The flowers will stay fresh longer because the stems will be able to get more water. **Splashes of Color:** Pink tulips look terrific in this green vase, but the large assortment of colors available makes tulips a great choice for all sorts of arrangements.

"Filling a clear vase with lemons, limes, cranberries, or in this case green onions, helps hold the flower stems where you want them."

Kay Clarke

A bundle of calla lilies glistens in the sunshine. **Stem Secrets:** The clear container makes the stems part of the arrangement. Green onions are mixed in with the calla lilies as a decorative way to hold the flowers in place. **Sized to Perfection:** This vase is just the right scale for the bouquet of calla lilies, an important consideration when putting flowers together. **Impact with Color:** The mixture of vibrant yellow blooms and bright green stems works together to make a bold decoration.

Mixing flowers, candles, and fruits creates an imaginative centerpiece. **Great Gerberas:** Red gerbera daisies add a playful element to the arrangement. Wrap thin floral wire around the long stems to give them support, if needed. **Iron Secret:** The iron container holds floral foam that has been soaked in water. Moistened floral foam provides water for the flowers and holds the stems in place. Moss tucked along the sides of the container hides the foam. **Fun Foundation:** Nestling pillar candles, red and green apples, and dill at the base of the centerpiece adds a unique design.

"*Moistened floral foam in a plastic bag keeps flowers in wire baskets fresh and easy to arrange.*" **Kay Clarke**

Let a basket filled with flowers from the garden designate the seat of honor. **Fancy Free:** A piece of floral foam tucked inside a wire basket lined with moss ensures that this arrangement stays fresh. A plastic bag holds the foam and contains the moisture. An alternative is to place a glass container filled with water and flower food in the basket. **Long Live the Bloom:** To help blooms stay fresh, condition them right after they're cut. Place cut flowers in a bucket of water so the stems can draw as much water as possible.

enchanting
buffets

Setting an attractive buffet table can be a fun way to show your entertaining style. Keep in mind that not everything has to match. Unusual combinations of colors and materials offer a lot of creative freedom. To spark your imagination, search your closets and cupboards for favorite pieces. Here are some ideas to consider.

• Baskets, trays, and pastry tiers are versatile serving pieces.

• Mix and match several kinds of glasses for added interest. Sparkling stemware can also be used to hold small floating candles.

• Punch bowls are not just for punch. Fill a large bowl with ice to hold beverages in bottles and cans. Wreathe the base of the bowl with greenery and flowers.

• Incorporate a favorite collection, such as large shells or miniature boxes, into the table setting.

• Use pitchers, soup tureens, even teapots as creative floral containers.

Ashley Wyatt
Photo Stylist, *Cottage Living*

When entertaining outdoors, use candles, glass jars, and fresh cuttings for a creative table setting that reflects the warm tones of a sunset. **Simple Elegance:** The secret to the beautiful glow is grouping lots of candles and clear jars with linens and flowers in oranges and yellows. **Size Wise:** Combine cream candles and glass containers in various shapes and sizes. **Fresh Flowers:** Simple arrangements of seasonal blooms add a lighthearted mood. Bear grass jutting out from tall bottles gives height at one end of the table. **Set a Light Mood:** Jars holding flatware are nestled among stacks of light-colored plates and bowls. Using clear containers keeps the look airy and upbeat.

Set up buffets in several areas for easy flow.
Crowd Control: Use more than one table or sideboard to arrange buffet items. This is an especially good idea when you have a large number of people in a small space. For example, place plates and flatware in one area and food in another. **Flower Flair:** Accent the buffet with bowls and vases filled with fresh flowers. **Common Denominator:** Enhance the decorating theme by repeating similar elements. Here, the rooster-motif centerpiece and wall sconces set a whimsical mood.

A sideboard filled with fragrant flowers provides the perfect spot for a sampling of desserts. **Take a Stand:** Elevating the cake on a pedestal makes it a key feature of the sideboard decoration. Wired silk ribbon trimming the plate of petit fours beautifully frames the miniature cakes. **Good Reflections:** Flowers, greenery, and candles can always be counted on to make a setting special. Arranging them in front of a mirror doubles the effect.

A few simple embellishments set the stage for a casual Italian supper. **Perfect Pasta:** Glass urns filled with various types of pasta and coordinating candles create an easy, imaginative display. **Breadstick Vase:** A clear urn makes a clever container for breadsticks and mirrors the containers filled with pasta and candles. **Playful Pottery:** A few pieces of brightly colored Italian pottery mixed among earth-toned bowls complete the informal setting.

A vibrant table runner is an excellent complement to colorful pottery plates and adds a festive look to the table setting. **Less Is More:** Several plate stands used as serving pieces make good use of table space by allowing more food to be presented at one time—minimizing repeated refills by the hostess. **Looks Count:** Creative placement of food on serving plates makes a good first impression for guests and gives the food even more appeal. **In the Middle:** A simple pitcher filled with loosely arranged flowers is an easy finishing touch. Flowers make any setting more special.

This colorful wall arrangement means table-top decorations can be kept to a minimum. **Set for Style:** Beautiful plates and ironwork provide an interesting stage for this dessert buffet. The plates and chargers are attached to the wall with ordinary plate hangers. Cling tape clips the hanger used on the plate to the charger and is then concealed with ribbon. **At Your Service:** Serving pieces in varying heights, colors, and shapes combine for an elegant buffet on a dining room sideboard. Candles are a must for every festive occasion.

"Bright colors always delight the eye and add to the excitement of a setting." **Ashley Wyatt**

Playful punches of color add fun to a coffee-and-dessert table. **Tray Chic:** A decorative tray is ideal for transporting desserts and other accessories to the table and keeping things organized once there. **Pretty Pillars:** A ring of miniature flowers jazzes up a pair of pillar candles resting on decorative candlesticks. **Don't Spill the Beans:** Coffee beans fill small glass containers and provide a sturdy foundation for bright gerbera daisies.